Rooibos Revolution

Recipes for Nature's Healing Tea

Sally Errey

Rooibos Revolution

Recipes for Nature's Healing Tea

by

Sally Errey

First Edition

Belissimo Books
Vancouver, Canada

Rooibos Revolution

Recipes for Nature's Healing Tea

Sally Errey

First Published in 2005 by:
Belissimo Books
Box 46838, Vancouver, British Columbia
V6J 5M4, Canada

Every effort has been made to ensure that the information contained in this book is complete and accurate. However, neither the publisher nor the author is engaged in rendering professional advice or services to the individual reader. The ideas, procedures, and suggestions contained in this book are not intended as a substitute for consulting a physician or health care professional. All matters regarding your health require responsible supervision.

The purpose of this book is to educate and entertain. Neither the author nor the publisher shall be liable or responsible for any loss, injury, or damage allegedly arising from any information or suggestion in this book.

It is recommended the recipes contained in this book be followed as written. The author and publisher are not responsible for your specific health or allergy needs that may require medical supervision. The author and publisher are not responsible for any adverse reactions to the recipes contained in this book.

Library and Archives Canada Cataloguing in Publication Data
Errey, Sally

Rooibos revolution : recipes for nature's healing tea / Sally Errey.
ISBN 0-9732987-2-3
1. Rooibos tea. 2. Cookery (Tea) I. Title.
TX817.T3E77 2005 641.6'372 C2004-905257-8
Printed in Canada

Editor: Sandra Tonn
Photographer: Edmond Fong
Art Director: Terence Yeung
Food Stylist: Sally Errey

Table of Contents

Foreword

Rooibos tea has been consumed by South African communities for centuries. Even before today's scientific interest in the healing qualities of Rooibos, a wealth of anecdotal evidence has provided important information about the use of this unique herbal beverage in relation to health and healing.

Chemically, the major antioxidant constituents differ from green and black teas. In addition, the natural absence of caffeine and its low tannin content contributes to the popularity of Rooibos tea as a health beverage.

The key health benefits of Rooibos tea established thus far include (i) the beneficial effects it has shown, in test tube and animals studies, to prevent cancer; (ii) the beneficial enhancement of the body's liver enzymes that play an important role in preventing cancer; and (iii) an increase in beneficial and disease-fighting antioxidants in the liver of rats.

Can the present data and benefits be extrapolated to humans? Time will tell. It is well documented that mutations in somatic cells lead to the induction of cancer. It is the hope, then, that the above named benefits will prove beneficial in humans.

Results from our studies at *the Program on Mycotoxins and Experimental Carcinogenesis* in South Africa, and others from around the world, strongly suggest that the consumption of Rooibos tea may play a role in improving our overall health, and may also alleviate the burden of cancer in our community.

On a personal note, I have consumed it since childhood. I can still remember the pleasant aroma of Rooibos tea wafting from the kitchen of my grandparents, who always had a pot brewing on the stove. Nowadays there are many different ways of consuming Rooibos, and I prefer the iced tea version for summer while nothing beats a hot cup of Rooibos tea before bedtime. For variety I mix it with my favorite fruit juices, such as orange or berry. It is also very refreshing with a slice of lemon.

I believe in consuming Rooibos tea in its natural form, as an aqueous infusion, and am weary of concentrated supplements. I am delighted to admit that, after reviewing the delicious recipes in this book, that even I didn't know one could do so much with Rooibos!

I am very excited about the results obtained with Rooibos tea and our focus at the Research Unit will continue to be dedicated to the discovery of its health protecting mechanisms. Ultimately, we will conduct human studies. There is still a lot brewing in the Rooibos pot for us all to discover and explore—and taste!

Jeanine L Marnewick
Senior Research Scientist
PROMEC Unit
Medical Research Council of South Africa

Introduction

My first exposure to Rooibos tea was when I was working with a South African colleague, who raved about a wonderful tea from her homeland. As a stressed-out, coffee-drinking computer professional at the time, I wasn't too interested in giving this healing tea a try.

As time moved on, my career moved into the field of nutrition, optimal health, cancer prevention and disease management. In my regular health seminars to cancer patients, I spoke about the benefits of black and green tea in cancer management. More and more people started asking me about the caffeine-free Rooibos tea. They'd tried it, loved the taste and heard all the claims of its healing properties. They wanted to know: Were all the health claims about his tea true? I wanted to know the same thing.

After months of asking around for Rooibos information I finally crossed paths with Liz Bandelin, owner of Nu-tea (www.nu-tea.com), who offered me some samples of her pure red and green Rooibos varieties. Did she have the background science on the claims? You bet, and so I started my love affair with Rooibos in both healing potential and taste.

Studies to date have only been conducted on animals or in the test tube, however they show great promise as we learn more about the antioxidants and other powerful plant nutrients in the tea. It's only a matter of time until studies with humans are conducted and we learn more about this ancient herbal brew.

In the meantime, I have become a willing guinea pig, brewing up a few cups of tea each morning to use throughout the day in frozen frappés if it's hot and sunny, in warming winter drinks if it's chilly, or by simply adding it as an ingredient to my evening meal.

If you haven't tried this magical tea, get ready for the Rooibos Revolution.

All about Rooibos

Rooibos tea is the national beverage of South Africa. Take a flight on South African Airways, or ask at any home or café and it will be served up fresh and steaming. Pronounced *Roy-Boss*, the name translates to "Red Bush," which is a small flowering shrub indigenous to the Western Cape of South Africa. The refreshing brew imparts a hearty flavour with subtle vanilla tones, and contains no caffeine and very little tannins. The low tannin content means there is no bitter or astringent taste, which makes the tea ideal for cooking.

The Rooibos bush provides the leaves for the tea. (By strict definition it is a herbal "tisane" or infusion, but common use of the word "tea" now extends to many herbal preparations.) The leaves are picked, fermented and dried. This is the red type of Rooibos, which brews a deep, rich red colour. The change in polyphenol composition is the reason the tea changes colour with fermentation. There is also a non-fermented "green" Rooibos available, which is equally delicious and contains even more healthful properties. It is a light honey colour when brewed.

History of Rooibos

The unique Rooibos bush only grows in the arid, hilly region of the Cedarburg Mountains in South Africa. It was first used as a healing beverage hundreds of years ago by the indigenous peoples who would pick the leaves and stems, break them with wooden hammers, ferment them in small heaps and then dry them in the sun.

Little has changed as South Africans have moved into modern production. The same steps are taken, but of course up-to-date machinery is used. Production and exports have grown substantially as more and more people around the world enjoy the taste and benefits of Rooibos. The tea is currently exported to Australia, Canada, China, England, Germany, Japan, Holland, South Korea, Malaysia, Poland and the United States.

A high level of quality control ensures that all exported Rooibos products pass inspections and are certified to be free of bacteria and impurities by the Perishable Products Export Control Board of South Africa. Rooibos is then graded according to flavour, cut-length and colour with "supergrade" being the highest designation of quality. Organic Rooibos is also available.

The Rooibos leaves are quite small. As a result they work well as both a bulk loose leaf and in tea bags. Either way, the tea may still be "supergrade" and of high quality. (In other commercial tea operations, tea bag contents often contain tea of inferior quality.)

Traditional Healing Remedies

Rooibos has a long and varied history of use in South Africa for a variety of ailments. While its healing properties may not be fully or scientifically proven as of yet, it is always worthwhile to note the cultural wisdom and anecdotal evidence of traditional remedies. In fact, science has discovered many modern medicines by observing the use of healing plants by other cultures. Once identified, researchers isolate the active, or healing, chemical ingredients in the plant.

Fortunately, Rutgers University provides a quality control program for local growers, evaluating factors such as pH, moisture content, cleanliness, total flavonoid content, and antioxidant capability for tea samples collected from both the industry in general and from specific areas. Data from their analyses are made available and help us understand why the tea may assist in healing a variety of complaints.

Flavanoids are a group of chemical compounds naturally found in certain fruits, vegetables, teas, wines, nuts, seeds and roots. Although not considered vitamins, flavonoids have a number of nutritional functions that modify chemical reactions in the body. Most act as antioxidants, and some have anti-inflammatory properties.

Allergies and Hayfever

Rooibos tea is considerably high in special antioxidants called flavonoids. Flavonoids, particularly quercetin and rutin, have been shown in separate studies to have anti-inflammatory properties and help reduce histamine release and the allergic response. Drinking the tea on a daily basis could help considerably.

Skin Complaints

The presence of phenolic carboxylic acids (such as alpha-hydroxy acid) may be the reason Rooibos helps improve condition and heal the skin when applied topically. These compounds have anti-fungal and anti-bacterial properties, and also act as mild antioxidants. Traditionally, Rooibos has been used for eczema, dermatitis, acne, diaper rash and sunburn. It can be applied topically (simply brew the tea and apply) and has also been shown to improve skin conditions when taken internally.

A study at the Aichi Medical University in Japan established that patients with dermatitis showed a significant decrease in their itching when drinking Rooibos tea. Similarly, acne and psoriasis sufferers showed a marked improvement after drinking the tea, as did those with recurrent Herpes simplex.

Digestion Problems

Rooibos tea contains the flavonoids luteolin and quercetin, which have anti-spasmodic effects. This may explain why Rooibos works, and is generally recommended by South African physicians and nurses, for colic in babies. It may also help with nausea and in easing other digestive complaints.

Insomnia

It has been claimed that Rooibos helps with insomnia and promotes restful sleep. It is certainly used successfully in this way by the general public in South Africa. Studies have yet to indicate any active ingredients that may assist with relaxation, but as a caffeine-free beverage it certainly has no stimulatory effects.

Electrolyte Replacement

Rooibos contains several minerals including calcium, copper, naturally occurring fluoride, magnesium, manganese, zinc and the electrolytes potassium and sodium. While the minerals are present in trace amounts, if Rooibos is used as a fluid replacement throughout the day, as many athletes in South Africa use it, the tea can be considered a dietary source of minerals and help replace lost electrolytes after physical activity and sweating.

Chronic Degenerative Diseases

To understand chronic degenerative disease (disease that happens slowly, over time), we first need to understand antioxidants and free radicals. Free radicals are unstable molecules in our bodies that have lost an electron. These are so tiny, they can damage DNA cells, which can cause cancer and accelerate aging. Free radicals can also oxidize cholesterol, leading to clogged arteries and the potential for heart attack, high blood pressure and stroke.

Antioxidants help counteract free radicals, thus reducing the risk of disease and promoting health and cell longevity. Plants are high in antioxidants (often found in the polyphenol form) because they use these compounds as sunscreen, insect repellants and anti-bacterials. The term antioxidant is an umbrella term and within its scope fall the polyphenols, which then contain the flavonoid and phenolic acid families. These powerful compounds have been found in both red (fermented) and green (unfermented) Rooibos teas.

The types of polyphenols in Rooibos tea are different than those in traditional green and black teas, so the potential health benefits of the teas cannot be compared solely on their total polyphenol content. When total antioxidant activity and free radical inhibition between teas was measured by researchers, the differences were marginal. With green tea leading at 90.8 per cent inhibition, followed by unfermented green Rooibos at 86.6 per cent, fermented red Rooibos at 83.4 per cent and black tea at 81.7 per cent. Researchers still continue to find new polyphenols, in addition to other healing properties and nutrients, in Rooibos, therefore not all beneficial properties can be identified or quantified yet.

Heart Disease

Simply put, the flavonoids featured in Rooibos tea have a host of beneficial effects that could potentially help reduce the risk of coronary disease. The flavonoid rutin, for example, enhances the stability and permeability of capillary arteries. Quercetin, on the other hand, helps prevent the oxidation of LDLs ("bad" cholesterol) and may reduce fatty deposits in the arteries, reducing the risk of atherosclerosis and potential stroke and heart attack. Flavone Glycosides (natural plant sugar molecules) are also being studied in South Africa as they may lower blood pressure.

Cancer

As Jeanine L. Marnewick, Senior Research Scientist for the Medical Research Council of South Africa explained in her Foreword to the book, the key established benefits of Rooibos tea thus far appear extremely promising when it comes to cancer prevention.

Antioxidants are important to reduce DNA damage, the basis for most cancer formation. Some preliminary studies in test tubes and animals are indicating how powerful Rooibos's cancer fighting polyphenols may be.

One of these polyphenols is caffeic acid. In tests, caffeic acid was just as active as an antioxidant as the most potent flavonoids tested (quercetin, isoquercitrin, and aspalathin). Rooibos also contains these. In separate studies, these flavonoids have been shown to make cancer cells die (apoptosis), decrease primary pancreatic tumour growth (quercetin specifically) and also inhibit cancer cell proliferation (thyroid and colon cancer cells). While these ingredients are found in Rooibos tea, researchers are yet to investigate how much is absorbed in humans when consumed.

In other tests on free radical scavenging activity, five of the flavonoids found in Rooibos were more effective than the benchmark vitamin E.

Animal studies indicate that rutin and orientin, both found in Rooibos tea, may help reduce fat oxidization (fat hardening and destruction) during exposure to radiation and also reduced damage to bone marrow and the gastrointestinal tract.

When deliberately trying to induce mutagens (cancer causing agents) researchers found that Rooibos tea significantly reduced cancer-associated changes in animal cells. Rooibos showed a greater suppression of abnormal cells than did green tea. When the cells were exposed to two mutagens simultaneously, the highest concentration of Rooibos tea (1000 microgram/ml) completely inhibited the deviant cells, bringing their percentage down to the same levels of those cells not exposed to any mutagen agents at all.

Radiation is often a key cause of free radical damage and increased cancer risk. One research group discovered red Rooibos tea reduced cancerous transformation of mouse cells in test tubes exposed to x-rays.

Diabetes

There may be potential for Diabetes management through Rooibos tea's levels of luteolin, quercetin, isoquercetin and rutin flavonoids. These flavonoids inhibit an enzyme that can initiate diabetes-associated complications. Pharmaceuticals also try and target this enzyme to control diabetes. Rooibos tea may be providing this action naturally through flavonoids.

Rooibos contains pinitol, which is a nutrient compound, called inositol, that is found in plants. Researchers are considering the possibility that pinitol may carry out the work of insulin since it possesses hypoglycemic properties that affect the uptake of glucose.

Natural non-sugar based flavanones act as natural sweetener, contributing to the sweet taste of Rooibos and eliminating the need to add sugar or artificial sweeteners.

Anti-aging

As fats oxidize (lipid peroxidation) in the brain, neurons and cells can become damaged and contribute to age-related diseases such as senility and Alzheimer's disease. Studies on rats that were given red Rooibos daily (as much as they wanted), showed a greatly reduced lipid formation in specific areas of their brains, thus potentially reducing age-related disease.

In addition, research from an anti-aging institute in Japan showed that Rooibos tea has high concentrations of substances that *mimic* Superoxide Dismutase (SOD). (Please note that Rooibos does not contain SOD as some claims state). SOD is the enzyme in the human body that is most capable of neutralizing free radicals as soon as they are formed, which may help to explain the anti-aging benefits of Rooibos. Japanese researchers also found Rooibos tea to be beneficial in the treatment of liver diseases and cataracts.

At the time of writing, there are currently no known contra-indications or drug interactions for Rooibos tea.

Unfortunately, the mechanisms by which Rooibos produces its health giving benefits are still unclear because of a lack of detailed human studies. As more and more research is conducted on these antioxidants, the levels of them in Rooibos tea and the effects on human health, it will no doubt become a frequently enjoyed beverage worldwide.

Rooibos Reservations

Two claims often associated with Rooibos tea are with regard to helping fight the HIV/AIDS virus and that Rooibos has 50 times more antioxidants than green tea.

Currently, there's no evidence that Rooibos tea fights the HIV virus. One Japanese study found that a polysaccharide in Rooibos leaves may have antiviral activity against the HIV virus. However, that polysaccharide had to be chemically extracted from the leaves and is not found in drinking tea (steeping the leaves in hot water). Who knows if there is benefit in consuming the leaves as a whole ingredient - as suggested in some of the following recipes for marinades and sauces?

Many claims have been repeated on the Internet and in the media that Rooibos has 50 times the antioxidants of green tea. In actual fact, my research has not uncovered the source of this information. It does not appear in any of the abstracts or papers I have reviewed. I try and avoid comparing the two (Rooibos and Green tea) as they both have benefits and green tea has outstanding supporting data (including human studies) for its immune boosting, cancer fighting and anti-oxidant properties. As a nutritionist I fully recommend the benefits and regular consumption of both Rooibos and green tea.

Ready. Set. Rooibos.

Once you've experienced the fantastic flavour of Rooibos tea there's really no limit to how it can be used for everyday cooking or to add a gourmet flair.

For maximum antioxidant exposure and health benefits use the brewed tea instead of the water or stock called for in recipes, such as soups, stews, grains, pastas and sauces. As you'll see in the recipes section, Rooibos is also ideal for hot and cold drinks, and you can use the whole leaf in rubs and marinades.

You can even add a final garnishing touch to cold drinks with decorated Rooibos ice-cubes.

Adding Rooibos to favourite recipes gives them an original twist that will truly make it your very own, healthful, gourmet dish.

Where to Buy

Rooibos can be found in specialty tea stores, health food stores, in some supermarkets and on-line via the Internet. Ideally buy a brand that provides organic, "supergrade" leaves. The loose leaves and tea bags are one and the same, as the leaves are very small.

Preparation Guidelines

- Use one tea bag or 1 tablespoon of loose-leaf tea in an infuser for 4-5 cups of boiling water.
- Use 1 teaspoon of loose leaf for one cup of water.
- Steep for a minimum of 10 minutes for maximum colour, flavour and nutrition. Rooibos can brew even longer because its lack of tannins will not result in bitterness.
- Depending on how you like your tea, Rooibos blends well

with honey, maple syrup, milk or soy milk. Try it without any additions for the first few times to truly appreciate its subtle qualities.

Handy Hints

- Do not microwave your Rooibos tea. Initial studies on microwaves indicate that they may destroy flavonoid content. (The first studies done with broccoli, showed that 97 per cent of flavonoids were destroyed when the broccoli was cooked in the microwave.)
- When making your morning tea, simply make extra tea in a 4 cup Pyrex glass jug or large teapot. Allow to cool and use for drinks and to cook with as required.

Rooibos Blends

There are many different blends on the market that make for a delicious hot Rooibos beverage. All of the recipes in this book have been designed using the pure red (fermented) or green (unfermented) Rooibos teas for maximum flavour and health benefits.

Other South African indigenous teas include honeybush (with a lighter honey flavour) and buchu, which has limits on production and is more expensive. It has a heady floral aroma due to its essential oils and is often blended with Rooibos so as not to overwhelm flavour. Keep an eye out for these variations as they would be ideal for many of these recipes.

Feel free to experiment with any of your favourite Rooibos teas and blends. That's what these recipe ideas are all about!

Christmas Cranberry Rooibos Drink page 26

Green Ginger Rooibos Frappe page 30

South Pacific Shrimp or Tofu with Rooibos Sauce page 42

Blonde Poached Pears with Honeybush or Green Rooibos page 49

Rooibos Recipes

Hot Rooibos Tea Drinks

Christmas Cranberry Rooibos Drink

3 cups (750 ml) cranberry juice

¾ cup (180 ml) orange juice concentrate

3 cups (750 ml) Rooibos red tea, brewed

1 stick cinnamon

2 cloves

In a saucepan, or crockpot, combine all ingredients. Over medium heat warm through and lower temperature to simmer for 15 minutes. Remove cinnamon stick and cloves before garnishing.

Serves 6

Rooibos Sun Tea

1 tsp (5 ml) Rooibos red or green tea leaves

3 cups (750 ml) filtered water

¼ cup (60 ml) mint, crushed (or lavender or other fresh herbs)

2-4 Tbsp (30 – 60 ml) honey to taste

In a glass jar or pitcher, place 1 teaspoon of Rooibos tea or 1 tea bag in the water (with sweetener, if you wish). Cover and set in the sun for over an hour. Note: the water will not boil like regular tea.

Serves 2

Ginger Peachy Rooibos Tea

1 cup (250 ml) Rooibos green tea, brewed
1 cup (250 ml) peach juice
2 tsp (10 ml) lemon juice
1 tsp (5 ml) dried powdered ginger

In a saucepan, or crockpot, combine all ingredients. Over medium heat warm through and serve.

Serves 2

Rooibos Lavender Mint Tea

½ tsp (2 ml) dried lavender flowers
½ tsp (2 ml) Rooibos green tea, leaves
2 Tbsp (30 ml) fresh mint leaves or 2 tsp (10 ml) dried mint
1 cup (250 ml) boiling water
Honey to taste

In a teapot, combine the lavender flowers, Rooibos leaves and mint. Pour boiling water over the mixture. Steep for ten minutes. Serve hot or chilled.

Serves 1

Red Rooibos Party Tea

2 cups (500 ml) 100% cranberry juice
1 cup (250 ml) Rooibos red tea, brewed
1 cup (250 ml) apple juice

In a saucepan, or crockpot, combine all ingredients. Over medium heat warm through and serve.

Serves 4

Lemon Rooibos Detox Tea

1 cup (250 ml) Rooibos tea, brewed
1 Tbsp (15 ml) maple syrup or honey
Freshly-squeezed juice of half a lemon
Cayenne pepper to taste (sparingly)

Stir maple syrup, lemon juice and cayenne together in a cup. Fill with hot Rooibos tea and enjoy first thing in the morning.

Serves 1

Hot Red Grape and Rooibos Drink

1 cup (250 ml) Rooibos red tea, brewed
1 cup (250 ml) red grape juice
1 cinnamon stick
2 tsp (10 ml) honey
1 lemon, sliced

In a saucepan, or crockpot, combine all ingredients. Over medium heat warm through and serve. Garnish with lemon slices.

Serves 2

Bed Time Relaxation Tea

1 tsp (5 ml) Rooibos green tea, leaves
¼ cup (60 ml) dried chamomile flowers (optional)
¾ cup (180 ml) boiling water
¼ cup (60 ml) vanilla soy milk
Honey or maple syrup to sweeten

Pour boiling water over the chamomile and Rooibos leaves, cover, and steep 15 to 20 minutes, until strong. Add the soy milk and sweetener to taste.

Serves 1

Chilled Rooibos Drinks

- For these drinks consider using ice cubes made from strongly brewed Rooibos tea.
- Results are best if all ingredients are chilled.
- Depending on the ripeness and sweetness of the fruits used, some sweetener may need to be added to taste.
- For breakfast drinks, place all the ingredients in the blender and put in the fridge the night before. Simply blend in the morning for a super fast breakfast.

Banana Berry Rooibos Frappe

½ cup (125 ml) strawberries
½ cup (125 ml) blueberries
1 ripe banana
2 tsp (10 ml) honey
¼ tsp (1 ml) cinnamon
½ cup (125 ml) Rooibos tea, brewed, chilled
½ cup (125 ml) Rooibos ice cubes

Starting with the fruits, place everything in a blender. Pulse to chop the fruit and then blend until smooth. Serve immediately and garnish with mint or fruit pieces.

Serves 2

Pineapple & Mango Rooibos Bliss

1 cup (250 ml) fresh pineapple
½ cup (125 ml) fresh mango (or papaya)
½ cup (125 ml) Rooibos tea brewed, chilled
¼ cup (60 ml) guava juice
1 Tbsp (15 ml) lime juice
½ cup (125 ml) Rooibos ice cubes

Starting with the fruits, place everything in a blender. Pulse to chop the fruit and then blend until smooth. Serve immediately and garnish with mint or fruit pieces.

Serves 2

Green Ginger Rooibos Frappe

1 cup (250 ml) honeydew melon
½ cup (125 ml) green kiwi, peeled
½ ripe banana
½cup (125 ml) Rooibos green tea, brewed,chilled
¼ cup (60 ml) kiwi juice (available from specialty food stores)
2 tsp (10 ml) lime juice
2 Tbsp (30 ml) maple syrup or honey
1 cup (250 ml) Rooibos ice cubes

Starting with the fruits, place everything in a blender. Pulse to chop the fruit and then blend until smooth. Serve immediately and garnish with mint or fruit pieces.

Serves 2

Tropical Rooibos Cocktail

3 cups (750 ml) Rooibos tea, brewed, chilled
1 cup (250 ml) pineapple juice
1 cup (250 ml) crushed pineapple
¼ cup (60 ml) sweetener (optional)
2 cups (500 ml) crushed ice
Fresh mint, chopped

In a large pitcher, mix together the Rooibos, pineapple juice, sweetener and ice. Stir in pineapple pieces and mint.

Serves 4

Watermelon Rooibos Frappe

1 cup (250 ml) seedless watermelon, diced
½ ripe peach, diced
½ cup (125 ml) vanilla yogurt or soy equivalent
½ cup (125 ml) Rooibos tea, brewed, chilled
⅓ cup (85 ml) peach frozen yogurt
(see recipe page 50)

Starting with the fruits, place everything in a blender. Pulse to chop the fruit and then blend until smooth. Serve immediately and garnish with mint or fruit pieces.

Serves 2

Mango Rooibos Fruit Punch

2 cups (500 ml) strong, Rooibos tea, brewed chilled
1 cup (250 ml) apple juice
1 cup (250 ml) mango nectar
2 cups (500 ml) sparkling soda water, chilled
1 banana, sliced
1 cup (250 ml) strawberries, sliced
1 cup (250 ml) crushed pineapple
Sprigs of mint

In a large punch bowl, mix together the Rooibos and fruit juices. Add the soda water just before serving. Add the fruit pieces, garnish with strawberries and mint. Serve with icecubes.

Makes 6 cups

Rooibos Grape Frappe

½ cup (125 ml) Rooibos tea, brewed, chilled
1 cup (250 ml) red grape juice
1 cup (250 ml) vanilla frozen yogurt
½ cup (125 ml) seedless red grapes, skinned

Starting with the fruits, place everything in a blender. Pulse to chop the fruit and then blend until smooth. Serve immediately and garnish with mint or fruit pieces.

Serves 2

Tangy Grapefruit Roobois Blend

1½ cups (375 ml) sparkling apple juice, chilled
1 cup (250 ml) Rooibos tea, brewed chilled
1 cup (250 ml) unsweetened grapefruit juice, chilled
½ cup (125 ml) apricot nectar
½ cup (125 ml) mint, chopped
2 cups (500 ml) crushed ice

In a blender, add the mint and 1 cup of the ice. Blend well until the mint is very finely chopped. Mix Rooibos with sparkling apple juice, grapefruit and apricot juice. Add the mint and crushed ice.

Serves 4

Rooibos Iced Tea

4 cups (1L) Rooibos tea, brewed, chilled
1 cup (250 ml) orange juice
2 Tbsp (30 ml) lemon juice
⅓ cup (85 ml) natural ginger ale
1 orange, sliced
2 Tbsp (30 ml) fresh ginger, sliced

In a large pitcher, mix together the Rooibos, ginger slices and fruit juices. Add the ginger ale just before serving. Garnish with orange slices. Add ice if desired.

Makes 6 cups

Canteloupe & Apricot Rooibos Frappe

1 cup (250 ml) cantaloupe
½ cup (125 ml) fresh apricots
½ ripe banana
½ cup (125 ml) Rooibos tea, brewed, chilled
1 tsp (5 ml) lemon juice
1 – 2 tsp (5 - 10 ml) ginger, peeled and chopped
1 Tbsp (15 ml) honey
½ cup (125 ml) Rooibos ice cubes

Starting with the fruits, place everything in a blender. Pulse to chop the fruit and then blend until smooth. Serve immediately and garnish with mint or fruit pieces.

Serves 2

Honeydew and Grape Rooibos Spritzer

1 small honeydew melon
1 cup (250 ml) Rooibos tea, brewed, chilled
½ cup (125 ml) seedless green grapes
½ cup (125 ml) freshly squeezed lime juice
½ cup (125 ml) honey
2 cups (500 ml) sparkling water

Cut melon in half, scoop out seeds, peel, and cut into 1-inch cubes. Wash grapes well. Freeze melon and grapes for one hour.

Combine frozen melon and grapes with lime juice and honey in a blender. Puree until smooth, adding sparkling water as needed. Serve immediately.

Serves 4

Chilled Ginger Rooibos Delight

3 cups (750 ml) Rooibos green tea, brewed hot
2-3 inches fresh ginger, sliced and bruised
¼ cup (60 ml) sweetener, to taste
3 Tbsp (45 ml) lemon juice
Fresh mint

Add the ginger to the hot Rooibos and allow to steep for 5 minutes. Remove the ginger or pour the drink through a strainer and sweeten to taste. Chill, add lemon juice and serve in tall glasses with fresh mint for garnish. The drink is also delicious served hot in winter.

Serves 2

Rooibos Maple Almond Milk

3 cups (750 ml) Rooibos tea, chilled
¾ cup (180 ml) soaked almonds (8-12 hours)
1 Tbsp (15 ml) maple syrup
½ tsp (2 ml) vanilla extract

In a blender, combine 2 cups of the chilled Rooibos tea and the almonds. Blend well for 1 minute. Strain through a fine mesh strainer into a pitcher. Place the pulp back in the blender with the remaining cup of Rooibos tea. Repeat the blending and straining into the pitcher. Stir in the maple syrup and vanilla extract and stir well to combine. Discard the pulp. Keep refrigerated for 2 days. Use in smoothies and blender drinks.

Makes 3 cups

Rooibos Punch

2 cups (500 ml) orange juice
1 cup (250 ml) Rooibos tea, brewed, chilled
1 cup (250 ml) tropical fruit juice (pineapple, mango or guava)
2 peaches, peeled and finely diced
1 cup (250 ml) strawberries, diced
2 Tbsp (30 ml) lemon juice
1 cup (250 ml) fresh sprigs of mint
Ice cubes

In a large punch bowl, mix together Rooibos, orange and tropical juices. Place the strawberries and peaches in a small bowl. Mix with lemon juice. Add the fruit to the punch bowl and add ½ cup (125 ml) mint. Cover with plastic wrap and chill to allow flavours to mingle. Remove mint. Add ice cubes and garnish with the rest of the fresh mint.

Serves 4

Organic Rooibos Pear Spritzer

4 cups (1 L) organic pear juice
2 cups (500 ml) Rooibos tea, brewed, chilled
1 cup (250 ml) sparkling or soda water
1 pear, diced
1 lemon, sliced
Fresh mint

Mix Rooibos with pear juice, pear and sparkling water. Serve and garnish with mint and lemon slices.

Serves 8

Champagne and Rooibos Punch

4 cups (1 L) Rooibos tea, brewed, chilled
2 cups (500 ml) apricot nectar
2 cups (500 ml) pineapple juice
½ cup (125 ml) triple sec or other fruit liqueur
½ cup (125 ml) pineapple chunks
½ cup (125 ml) strawberries, sliced
1 bottle champagne or sparkling wine, chilled

In a bowl, mix the Rooibos, fruit juices, liqueur, pineapple chunks and strawberries. Chill well.

In a large punch bowl, add the fruit and Rooibos mixture and add the champagne or sparkling wine just before serving. Add Rooibos ice cubes (see below) and garnish with sprigs of mint.

Serves 20

Rooibos & Fruit Decorative Ice Cubes

4 cups (1 L) Rooibos red tea, brewed, chilled
2 cups (500 ml) fresh fruits, finely chopped
(strawberries, kiwi fruits, peaches, melon)
¼ cup (60 ml) fresh mint, chopped

Mix together the Rooibos tea and finely chopped fruits. Using decorative ice cube molds, pour in the mixture and freeze. Use in punch bowls for decoration (they will float) or use as ice in frappe and other blended drink recipes.

Marinades, Sauces, Chutneys

Rooibos Tea Barbeque Rub

2 tsp (10 ml) maple syrup
2 tsp (10 ml) ground coriander
1 tsp (5 ml) Rooibos red tea leaves
1 tsp (5 ml) ground cumin
½ tsp (2 ml) ground cardamom seed
¼ tsp (1 ml) coarse sea salt
2 drops hot sauce
2 tsp (10 ml) olive oil
3 - 4 Tbsp (45 - 60 ml) lemon juice (optional) use if basting tofu

Mix all ingredients together and use as a rub for approx 1 pound (450 g) of meat, fish or tofu for grilling. For best results with tofu, add the lemon juice and use a pastry brush to baste before grilling on a hot barbeque.

Makes ¼ cup (60 ml)

Rooibos Barbeque Sauce

1 5.5 ounce (156 ml) can tomato paste
½ cup (125 ml) Rooibos red tea, brewed
½ cup (125 ml) molasses
1 tsp (5 ml) liquid smoke
½ tsp (2 ml) cinnamon
½ tsp (2 ml) allspice
2 cloves garlic, pressed
2 Tbsp (30 ml) tamari soy sauce
1 Tbsp (15 ml) balsamic vinegar
Pinch cayenne

In a medium bowl, mix together the tomato paste, molasses and Rooibos tea.

Add the remaining ingredients and mix well.

Serve with grilled tofu, meats, veggie burgers or kebobs. Keep well refrigerated.

Makes 1½ cups (375 ml)

Rooibos and Red Wine Reduction

1 Tbsp (15 ml) extra virgin olive oil
1 onion, peeled and sliced
1 cup (250 ml) Rooibos red tea, brewed
1½ cups (375 ml) dry red wine
1 Tbsp (15 ml) red wine vinegar
1 Tbsp (15 ml) lemon juice
½ cup (125 ml) fresh parsley, finely chopped
3 tsp (15 ml) Italian herbs, dried
1 tsp (5 ml) sea salt to taste

In a pot, heat the olive oil, add the onions and Italian herbs. Cook for 5 minutes until onions are translucent and soft. Add the Rooibos tea, red wine, red wine vinegar, lemon juice, parsley and Italian herbs. Bring to the boil and reduce heat. Simmer for 30- 35 minutes. Allow to cool and use as a marinade for meats (3-4 hours), braise meats in it or marinade and baste Portobello mushrooms for the grill.

Makes 2 cups (500 ml)

Indian Rooibos Marinade

1 cup (250 ml) Rooibos tea, brewed hot
1 cup (250 ml) tomato sauce or ketchup
¼ cup (60 ml) tamari soy sauce
¼ cup (60 ml) peachy Rooibos chutney (page 41)
2 cloves garlic, finely chopped
1 tsp (5 ml) rosemary, fresh, chopped finely
½ tsp (2 ml) thyme, dried

Whisk together all the ingredients in a bowl. Use as a marinade for meats and tofu. Baste while cooking.

Asian Rooibos Marinade

½ cup (125 ml) Rooibos tea, brewed, hot
½ cup (125 ml) tamari soy sauce
3 Tbsp (45 ml) toasted sesame oil
2 Tbsp (30 ml) lemon juice
2 cloves garlic, minced
1 Tbsp (15 ml) fresh ginger, minced
1 small onion, chopped finely

Whisk together all the ingredients in a bowl. Use as a marinade for meats and tofu. Baste while cooking.

Peachy Honeybush Rooibos Chutney

¾ cup (180 ml) apple cider vinegar
½ cup (125 ml) honey
½ cup (125 ml) Rooibos Honeybush or Green tea, brewed
¼ cup (60 ml) red bell pepper, finely diced
¼ cup (60 ml) sweet white onion, finely diced
2 Tbsp (30 ml) fresh ginger, minced
1 cinnamon stick
1 Tbsp (15 ml) mustard seeds
2 large, under-ripe peaches, peeled and diced.

In a large pot, combine the brewed Rooibos tea, apple cider vinegar, honey, bell pepper, onion, ginger, mustard seeds and cinnamon stick. Bring to a boil over medium-high heat and boil for 5 minutes. Add the peaches, and reduce heat to simmer. Cook gently until the peaches are soft but hold their shape, about 5 minutes. Remove cinnamon stick. The chutney will thicken a little as it cools. Cool and place in sterilized jars. Stores for up to 3 weeks.

Makes 2 cups

Entrée Ideas with Rooibos

Braised and Spiced Tofu

2 Tbsp (30 ml) paprika
1 Tbsp (15 ml) Rooibos green tea leaves
2 tsp (10 ml) ground coriander
2 tsp (10 ml) ground cumin
2 tsp (10 ml) coarse sea salt
1 16 ounce (454 g) package of extra-firm Tofu
1 Tbsp (15 ml) extra virgin olive oil
¼ cup (60 ml) Rooibos, brewed hot
2 Tbsp (30 ml) lemon juice
4 tsp (20 ml) honey

In a small bowl, mix together the Rooibos green tea leaves, paprika, coriander, cumin and salt. Mix well with a small whisk. Drain Tofu and cut cross wise into 1 cm (½ inch) thick slices. Place the Tofu onto the spices, and flip, coating well on each side. Heat the oil, over medium-high heat, in a large non-stick skillet. Add the Tofu and cook on one side for 5 minutes. In a small bowl, mix together the hot Rooibos tea, lemon juice and honey. Flip the Tofu and cook for another 3 minutes. Add the liquid honey mixture to the pan and swirl to coat the Tofu. It will bubble up and evaporate a little. Serve hot.

Serves 4

South Pacific Shrimp or Tofu with Rooibos Sauce

¼ cup (60 ml) lime juice
⅓ cup (85 ml) light coconut milk
1 Tbsp (15 ml) Rooibos Honeybush or green leaves
2 tsp (10 ml) tamari soy sauce
1 tsp (5 ml) fresh ginger, minced
2 tsp (10 ml) red Serrano chilies, seeded and minced

1 Tbsp (15 ml) brown sugar
1 clove garlic, minced

1 16 ounce (454 g) package of extra-firm tofu OR
1 pound (454 g) shrimp, peeled and deveined

1 Tbsp (15 ml) extra virgin olive oil
½ cup (125 ml) tomato, seeded and diced
4 cups (1 L) baby spinach
1 tsp (5 ml) sea salt to taste
Fresh basil

In a large bowl combine the lime juice, coconut milk, Rooibos honeybush tea leaves, soy sauce, ginger , garlic, chiles, and brown sugar. Add the tofu or shrimp and toss well to coat. Marinate for 15 minutes in the refrigerator, stirring occasionally. Drain and reserve the marinade.

In a large skillet, heat the olive oil over medium-high heat. Add the tofu or shrimp and braise briefly until cooked (shrimp will be barely pink. Tofu will be light golden in colour). Remove from pan. Add the tomato and spinach to the pan. Stir and cook for 1 minute, until the spinach has turned bright green and wilted. Add the marinade saved earlier and simmer for 3 minutes. Return the shrimp or tofu, stir well and heat through. Add salt to taste. Serve immediately and garnish with fresh basil.

Serves 4

Pineapple Rooibos Sauce with Coconut

2 cups (500 ml) Rooibos tea, brewed
2 cups (500 ml) cooked organic chicken, veggie chicken strips or extra firm tofu, diced
2 Tbsp (30 ml) extra virgin olive oil
2 onions, diced
1 green pepper, diced
2 Tbsp (30 ml) arrowroot or cornstarch
1 cup (250 ml) vegetable stock
1 cup (250 ml) coconut milk
1 Tbsp (15 ml) fresh ginger, minced
1 14 oz can (398 ml) pineapple chunks, drained (save juice)
1 tsp (5 ml) sea salt (to taste)
¼ cup (60 ml) fresh cilantro, chopped
¼ cup (60 ml) shredded coconut, roasted

In a large skillet on medium heat, gently heat the olive oil. Add the onions and ginger and sauté for 5 minutes. Add the green peppers and continue to cook for another 5 minutes. In a small bowl, combine Rooibos tea and arrowroot powder. Add this Rooibos mix, coconut milk, vegetable stock, salt and pineapple juice. Stir thoroughly. Add the cooked chicken or tofu and simmer for 15 minutes.

Stir in the pineapple chunks. Serve over rice or other grains and garnish with chopped cilantro and shredded coconut.

Serves 4

Saute with Rooibos - Orange Reduction

⅓ cup (85 ml) flour
½ tsp (2 ml) sea salt
½ tsp (2 ml) ground black pepper
¼ tsp (1 ml) turmeric

1 16 ounce (454 g) package of extra-firm tofu, sliced or flounder or sole fillets
1 Tbsp (15 ml) extra virgin olive oil
⅓ cup (85 ml) shallot, finely diced
½ cup (125 ml) dry white wine (or brewed Rooibos)
1 Tbsp (15 ml) orange juice concentrate
1 cup (250 ml) Rooibos tea, brewed
2 Tbsp (30 ml) fresh parsley, finely chopped
1 Tbsp (15 ml) Dijon mustard
1 tsp (5 ml) sea salt to taste

In a shallow dish, combine the flour, salt, pepper and turmeric. Dredge the tofu or fillets in the mixture until they are well coated.

In a large non stick frying pan, heat the olive oil over medium-high heat. Add the tofu or fish and cook until lightly browned, about 5 minutes per side. Transfer to the serving plates and cover loosely with foil.

Keep the frying pan on the stove and add the shallots. Stir well and cook for 5 minutes until softened and brown. In a small bowl, mix together the orange juice concentrate and the Rooibos tea and set aside. Add the wine to the pan and simmer, gently scraping the pan. Cook for 2 minutes, until reduced. Add the orange juice and Rooibos mixture and mustard to the frying pan. Bring to a boil and simmer until the sauce thickens, about 5 minutes. Add salt to taste. Add the parsley, stir well and serve on top of the tofu or fish. Garnish with extra parsley.

Serves 4

Minestrone Rooibos Soup

2 cups (500 ml) Rooibos tea, brewed
2 cups (500 ml) vegetable stock
2 14 ounce (796 ml) cans crushed tomatoes
2 Tbsp (30 ml) tomato paste
1 large potato, cubed
1 onion, chopped
2 stalks celery, chopped
2 carrots, chopped
2 Tbsp (30 ml) Italian seasoning, fresh or dried
1 15 ounce (425 ml) can kidney beans
1 large zucchini, sliced
1 cup (250 ml) uncooked shell or rotini pasta
Salt and pepper to taste

In a large soup pot combine the Rooibos tea, vegetable stock, the tomatoes, tomato paste, potato, onion, celery, carrot, and Italian seasoning. Bring to a boil and reduce heat. Simmer for 15-20 minutes.

Stir in the beans, zucchini and pasta; simmer for 10 to 15 more minutes until the vegetables are tender. Season with salt and pepper. Serve with warm crusty peasant bread.

Serves 8

Rooibos Chick Pea Cous Cous

1½ cups (375 ml) Rooibos green tea, brewed and hot
1 cup (250 ml) whole wheat couscous
1½ cups (375 ml) fresh peas or tomatoes, diced
2 cups (500 ml) chick peas, drained
½ cup (125 ml) parsley, chopped
2 Tbsp (30 ml) fresh basil, chopped
2 Tbsp (30 ml) fresh mint, chopped
1 Tbsp (15 ml) extra virgin olive oil
1 tsp (5 ml) fresh lemon zest, chopped
1 tsp (5 ml) sea salt
1 tsp (5 ml) fresh ground black pepper

In a large steel or tempered glass bowl, add the hot tea and couscous. Stir and cover for 10 minutes. Lightly steam the fresh peas (if using). Fluff the couscous with a fork and add peas (or tomatoes), chickpeas, parsley, mint, basil, olive oil, lemon zest and salt and pepper. Toss lightly

Serves 4

Creamy Mediterranean Rooibos Grilled Salmon (or Tofu)

¼ cup (60 ml) Rooibos tea, brewed
2 Tbsp (30 ml) natural or soy mayonnaise
¼ cup (60 ml) fresh parsley, chopped
¼ cup (60 ml) fresh basil, chopped
3 cloves garlic, minced
2 Tbsp (30 ml) lemon juice
1 Tbsp (15 ml) extra virgin olive oil
2 tsp (10 ml) Rooibos tea leaves
1½ tsp (7 ml) paprika
1 tsp (5 ml) ground cumin
1 tsp (5 ml) salt
4 salmon fillets OR
4 slices of extra firm tofu

In a small bowl, whisk together the mayonnaise, Rooibos tea, parsley, basil, garlic, oil, lemon juice, Rooibos tea leaves, paprika, cumin and salt. Set aside ¼ cup (60 ml) of the mixture. In a shallow dish, place the fillets of fish, or tofu piece on the bottom and cover with the remaining sauce. Marinate and refrigerate for 30 minutes, shaking occasionally to coat.

Heat the grill to medium heat. Remove the salmon or tofu and grill gently for 5 minutes on each side. Serve with the additional sauce set aside and a fresh salad.

Serves 4

Dreamy Rooibos Desserts

Blonde Poached Pears with Honeybush or Green Rooibos

4 cups (1 L) Rooibos Honeybush or green tea, brewed
½ cup (125 ml) apple juice concentrate
1 Tbsp (15 ml) crystallized ginger, chopped
½ tsp (2 ml) pure almond extract
4 Anjou or Bosc pears, firm, ripe, peeled, halved and cored.
¼ cup (60 ml), sliced almonds, toasted

In a large pot, heat the brewed tea, apple juice concentrate, ginger and almond extract until just boiling. Add the pear halves so that they have the cut side facing up. Poach over low heat for about 10 minutes or until tender, when they can be pierced easily with a skewer. Transfer the pears and the liquids to a bowl and allow to cool.

Serve the pears at room temperature, adding a little of the liquid. Garnish with toasted almonds.

Serves 4

Chocolate Rooibos Passion Sorbet

4 cups (1 L) water
4 Tbsp (60 ml) Rooibos tea leaves
1 cup (250 ml) unsweetened Dutch cocoa
¾ cup (180 ml) sugar
1 ounce (28 g) bittersweet chocolate, finely chopped

Bring the water to boil in a large pot. Using an infuser ball, add the tea (or 4 tea bags). Remove from the heat, cover and allow to steep for 20 minutes.

Remove the tea infuser or bags and return the pot to the stove. On medium-high heat, whisk the cocoa powder in slowly and then the sugar. Bring to a boil, reduce heat to simmer and cook for 20 minutes, until the mixture gets slightly thicker.

Take the pot off the heat and slowly stir in the chocolate until completely melted. Cover and chill in the refrigerator for 2 hours.

Transfer the mixture to an ice-cream maker and follow manufacturers instructions. If you desire it firmer, freeze for another 30 minutes after removing from the ice-cream maker.

Serves 8

If you don't have an ice-cream maker: Freeze sorbet mixture in a shallow metal baking pan until solid. Break into chunks and blend in a food processor until smooth and serve immediately.

Rooibos and Peach Frozen Yogurt

6 very ripe peaches, skins on, halved
1 cup (250 ml) Rooibos tea, brewed
⅔ cup (175 ml) brown sugar (or honey) to taste
1 Tbsp (15 ml) orange juice concentrate
2 cups (500 ml) thick or creamy vanilla yogurt (or soy yogurt)
2 Tbsp (30 ml) honey

In a medium pot, combine the brewed Rooibos tea, orange juice concentrate, sugar and peach halves. Bring to boil over medium-high heat and stir well. Reduce heat to medium –low and cook for around 10 minutes, until the peaches skins loosen. Allow the mixture to cool a little and remove the peach skins and discard.

Cover and refrigerate the peaches and liquid and chill for 2 hours.

Stir the yogurt and honey into the peach mixture. Blend well in a food processor or blender.

Transfer the mixture to an ice-cream maker and follow manufacturers instructions.

Serves 8

If you don't have an ice-cream maker: Freeze sorbet mixture in a shallow metal baking pan until solid. Break into chunks and blend in a food processor until smooth and serve immediately.

Rooibos Stewed fruits

4 cups (1 L) apples, cherries, pears, plums, peaches or apricots, halved and pits removed.
¼ - 1 cup (60-250 ml) dried fruits such as prunes, raisins or cranberries
½ -1 cup (125 - 250 ml) Rooibos tea, brewed

Peel, core and slice apples or pears, but not too thinly. Place the cut fruits with the dried fruit in a pot. Add enough Rooibos tea to cover, and simmer until the apples and pears are just tender. Add a dash of cinnamon and honey to taste.

Serves 2 - 4

Radical Rooibos Popsicles

1 12 ounce can (355 ml) 100% fruit juice concentrate
4 cups (1 L) Rooibos tea, brewed hot

In a large pitcher, mix together the brewed Rooibos and fruit juice concentrate until thoroughly blended. Pour into popsicle containers or use wax paper cups and wooden sticks and freeze.

Serves 12

Cherry Pancake and Waffle Topping with Rooibos

½ cup (125 ml) Rooibos tea, brewed
¼ cup (60 ml) honey
2 Tbsp (30 ml) cornstarch or arrowroot powder
4 cups (1 L) frozen or fresh tart cherries
(such as a choke cherry)
1 tsp (5 ml) almond extract

Add the brewed Rooibos tea to a medium saucepan. Add the honey and cornstarch and mix well. Bring the mixture to a boil over medium heat. Stirring well until thickened. Add the cherries and almond extract and heat until the cherries are hot and soft.

Serve on pancakes of waffles, or store in canning jars in the freezer.

Makes 4 cups

About the Author

Sally Errey, RNCP, is an acclaimed international speaker on optimum health and longevity through healthy nutrition and lifestyle choices. Her 17 years of experience, combined with her love of food is reflected in her being the Food Editor and Food Stylist for *Alive* magazine and Nutrition Expert for *Canada's Healthy Living Guide*, as well as the Resident Nutritionist on Shaw TV's *Studio 4*. Sally is frequently invited to appear at Health Shows and Food Festivals.

Her company, Simple Nutrition Solutions, provides consulting services for those people seeking to manage and prevent illnesses such as diabetes, heart disease, arthritis and cancer. Sally is author of *Staying Alive! Cookbook for Cancer Free Living. Real Survivors…Real Recipes...Real Results*. (Belissimo Books, 2004).

Drawing on her experience of the body's immense capacity to heal, she brings vitality, a sense of adventure and humour to the field of nutrition.

Sally also provides services at the Centre for Integrated Healing, a Canadian national model for providing complementary care and alternative options for those living with cancer. Her lectures, weekly cooking classes and consultations have helped to transform many people's lives.

Sally is a humorous, informative and entertaining presenter and is available to share her knowledge with your group in a seminar or cooking demonstration setting.

To contact Sally, E-mail: happytummy@shaw.ca or
phone (604) 734-7125 ext 234.
Visit www.myhappytummy.com

Consultations are available in person or by phone.
Contact Sally today to book your appointment.

Rooibos Revolution ISBN # 0-9732987-2-3	USD Price each*	CDN Price each*	Shipping
1 copy	$11.95 USD	$14.95 CDN	$3.00
2 copies	$11.95 USD	$14.95 CDN	$ 6.00
3 copies	$11.95 USD	$14.95 CDN	$ 7.00
Add $3 shipping for each of your first 2 books, then $1 per copy for additional orders.			

Total Number of Books ______ x $ ________ Subtotal $___________

Canadian Customers Please Add GST to Subtotal x 7 % Tax $___________

Please add the appropriate amount of shipping Shipping $___________

TOTAL$___________

Payment Method

❑Master ❑Visa Credit Card No: ______________________________ Expiry. ___/___

❑Cheque (payable to Belissimo Books)

Name: ____

Shipping Address: ____

City: ______________________Prov/State:______________________Postal/Zip: ______________

Tel:______________________eMail:______________________

Belissimo Books is based in Vancouver Canada. All credit card payments will be charged in the Canadian dollar equivalent.
GST will be charged for Canadian customers. Orders are processed once payment is received.
Print and Fax to: **1 (604) 648-9436 (toll free)** Phone Orders: **Call toll free 1 (877) 892-5483**
Mail with payment to: **Belissimo Books, Box 46838, Vancouver BC V6J 5M4, CAN**